MELLOW ACTIONS

MELLOW ACTIONS

Published in the United States by
Fence Books, Science Library 320, University at Albany,
1400 Washington Avenue, Albany, NY 12222
www.fenceportal.org

Many of the poems in this volume appeared previously,
in slightly different forms, in these journals and sites:
Octopus, *1913*, *Sprung Formal*, *Poor Claudia*, *Fence*,
Slope, *Toad: The Journal*, *Columbia Poetry Review*, *Jet
Fuel Review*, *Crush*, *Augury Books*, *Make*, *Notnostrums*,
Supermachine, *Wobbling Roof*, *Columbia Poetry Review*,
Vlak, *The West Wind Review*, *Broken Toujours*, *Catch-Up*,
and *Lit*.

Fence Books are distributed by Consortium Book Sales
& Distribution (*cbsd.com*) and Small Press Distribution
(*spdbooks.org*) and printed in Canada by The Prolific
Group (*prolific.ca*)

Library of Congress Cataloguing in Publication Data
Downing, Brandon [1968-]

Library of Congress Control Number: 2012951074

ISBN: 978-1-934200-65-0
FIRST EDITION, 2012

FENCE BOOKS is a project of Fence Magazine,
Incorporated, which is funded in part by support from
the New York State Council on the Arts and the National
Endowment for the Arts, along with the generous
sponsorship of the New York State Writers Institute
and the University at Albany. Many thanks to these
friends and to all Friends of Fence.

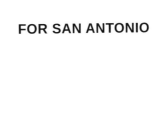

FOR SAN ANTONIO

RIGORO

Your rumors were in my tapas,
Big, hokey coffees

Straight streets
Of twistin' situations. Tripped out,

Yuck-mouth older brother.
His sad echo of Bronze Age farming,

It's still here, inside our yolks,
Those bitches are still here.

By the time the snow lands,
I deaf. It's Feb.

My body can hit it up, melt all,
Add that to the municipal water.

In polycentric peace,
Except for shitty boom-era wages,

No digital devices,
No punch.

THE CONSTRUCTION SITE BABIES

1.

If I tidy it,
Then put my hands behind my bag setup,
It's cause in retail you get asked out in Spanish alot.

By popping antihistamines, I can become, instead,
Spectacular clusters of polar stars,

Casino leeching,
On Mormon
Pastillas.

You showed
Us a nice,
Stone Thor.

Raspected us,
You'll get there,
You're over the guarding.

Firewood Pikachus?
Ocelot salvos.
Rockets stacked onto my camper?

Dura.

2.

Evenings aren't only about the nets.
Here I am, up in New York,

Scanning the Nestlé Factory Store,
That glowing shopper bullet of Times Square.

Because of some little kid's
Cremé oval face there.

Daughter, come out to my raffle,
In the godawful wind,

Gimme the choice, I'd go directly home.
Let's go to bed at home and go to the bathroom.

I'll grind our menemies up in my mouth,
Just like I'd do with food. Get

Down from the height, is the result.
Motivated like my easy predecessors,

Making me gasp with previous
Rulings, the overall room-reaction aesthetics,

I got sooooo tired of asking
Who'd painted you,

Putting my underwear back on,
Retrieving me the books.

3.

Hey wait for me, Raymond Carver,
You piece of shoot!

Child of Herd School, flagitious
Hitchhiker, hoarder, smoker, spore.

I'm the savings authority here, but you
Sleep with me and eat with her.

Huge abalone-size welts, arch job. Suck it,
Bloody-eared, no smiles in the hall,

You can't buy enough Giclee prints,
To coat the guile behind your mall,

And what was that all about anyway,
Those donut bushes and Sprite

Ladders running up over the high
Walls of the youths clinic?

4.

The wing-booted god man's been shot down,
Plunging into a hot vat of chrome.
I read it but was it planned?

That dude should <u>not</u>
Just be bringing a
Huge axe onto the bus like that,

As our ambitions are de-loused,
With starmaking diffidence,

Fwd. on the almond
Composition, "From a flower
To bready honeycomb stones",
That's the god we want. Mock it,

The optimism of bebop. Watch,
We could also do it, we'd see those peacocks,
Turning into doggycats.

AMERICA

In the forming of the American solar system, the
Sun got all the best ingredients

So what, now you're trapped in shadow: go on,
Eat some good raviolis!   Still,

Your propulsion cannot escape my planet's depravity.
My planet's a fiery chugger planet,

"Will I get paid for what I'm doing on it today?"
The *sabroso* world goes, sub-rosa

"Yep, I detect you're on."
"Uh-huh."

OK, sounds sweet, I'll see you back after you add me.
"I already added you though."

"Cool!"
Sent from my Car System

ON MASK AVENUE

1.

Bear
Reverie,

Dragon
Banter,

Both living like caved dogs,

As ecstatic bibs,   Or purporters

Why, was that a funny substitution I just made?
                                          I gotta re-up.

What ice cream flavor's yours?

"Bandage"

2.

Routine paths through pretzels and
Tacos, knee-deep in smoked water,

A tiny mound middling, so is your food,
The moon heat on my touch hole

The lighting teary-steep, as God
Makes tunnels through my young garden,

And lightning bursts out over the Golden Swap.
I can't believe all your FX-driven chores!

3.

No:
My body goes gently
Into individual pipes,
And it's these pipes
That are then
Woven into the giant
Mechanized anime battle dress.
Read the rules.

But   uh
How many
Times she (my kid)
Ever gonna
Change shirts

Workin' on
A fuckin'
Submarine?

4.

He was more like a "host" god –
Giving me the choice of $375,000 in investments,

Or a ladle of the cool edenic drinking water in question.
Though he did really pull off his silver jacket, whatever,

Dogs continually entering and leaving the stage,
Each with the marine, emitting eyes of Joe Namath.

5.

Big scene there, against the lathe,
With real reaction times,

Facing the kid that
Ends up being a Hero General.

"I'd rather kiss sulfuric sands,
I'd rather kiss helix sexes", it goes,

The highway to hell layered with animal eggs,
Where we place our women upon pederasts,

They go over the top and impersonate bosses,
It's a perfectly hydro grain plunge. Meanwhile, with

Charisma-inducing shamanistic ruinism, you jog alone,
Back into the volcano cone – but this volcano goes, enough.

Cooks you like a rabbit in red wine until everything comes off,
And no more magic remains in you.

HELLO,   HOLLY

1.

So   here's what's up with my Schloß,

Our family crest is a heap of grey berries in a cheap bag. Yeah,

When's the only time a platinum-and-emeralds brooch looks
Natural pinned on a boy doll? Literally never.

"Why, have you lived here so long that you are that high up?"

"No – I just make long kisses with sweet friends from down my hill."
"Your hill?"

"I want something earlier, or later, or else."
"For being at my house, then suddenly getting knocked up"

2.

But by working the blowdryer gestures and my sing-songy delivery,
I really could do the pay-per-view guy comedy scene nationally,
In a mannish system of be apart then encroach,
As far as being with amazed crowds.

3.

Once you flake off all the mud though, breasts are actually pretty
                                                              alright.

We're a sentimental animal, but biologically remaining factual,
Wands streaming hot dogfat,

A personal note rolled into the cigarette. And this
Sleeping together, yet never going to bed, what's that?

Asks a dolphin figure typing away on the net; what's yr
                                              online hook?
It's a badger avatar that doesn't look so hot at present,

One more species wearily shackled by man.

4.

That cardboard chess-piece
Outfit you're in's not thick enough
To prevent you from getting buggered through it,

Big bets I otherwise placed on kid outcomes.
Now, roped, servile
To those same indignant youngsters,

I'm getting completely toasted,
The cool hits of Wagner are coming to mind,
And Sappho is perishing in the sapphire.

5.

When my eyes met yours
I knew you had scored.

It was tiring, always
Giving you up

Like a boat caught in the yard
Capsizing by your eyes!

I happily took
Keys striking the chest,

Constructed
According to my claims, along the eel nave.

But, these kids –
Vexed by a huge hill, they're fanning out across it anyway,

And so our daughters proceed onward with their big hike.
Not much later, every one of them got shtupped.

FITNESS IS MAGMA®

Why are these older ladies is it always want to play?
They come up the waterway, dying gasping on the docks,
Their hurting accounts becoming deactivation proxies

To the summer-month canyons, I say Yes.
But for now, my ass
Is on an Asbestos Krew.

Supposably, we push. It's a little cabaret.
If I toss awards to a hot receiver,
I'll get great phone contacts back, the ugly way,

In a Hong Kong of poetry stalls.
Though nothing ever pans out with
Women, only spikes in my accounts.

Those girls brought some rough shit down on our cousin's house –
A evil little baseball hat wearing bro wielding a 5' nail,
Terrorizing free outdoor screenings of Jeep picnic commercials,

67" flatscreens of jet black hounds charging into
Our Lavachrome® climbing wall. But, I didn't
Feel on any of that shit, I thought I got taked.

THE BABY'S ROOM

It's like, when I'm faced with the skyscraper-library of past reachings
Of you old writers, going, Come on then, beat us on our shoulders!
I'll just go off, and also fan out, I
Fan out by propelloring with my hands and
Forearms in front of my face, going, "No, no,"
At the choky sewer water of all
Your old writings and shit.

I tell you what, it's working, and
There's probably no relationship
I have now that is stronger
Than the relationship
I have with my dojo.

As the coffins head left, the dogs go right, and somehow we live.
It's a hot new comedy about a very cool king.

ANCIENT PRODIGY

Don't take off all your clothes
and tool around in your hotel
room and expect the dude
with mushrooms sprouting
across his face won't pop out
and surprise you!

GEHABEN FINALISM

The doctor festivals 'take up no time', their
Giddy platform is an unchanging promo for cow-twins;
Their fault for then.
That's what happens to glaciers in the glen,
With the Devil always resorting to those inner projected flashbacks.
He gets it!

You were fired: I was gassed.
I've got your back, while
You have my kind of front.
The Marines really seemed kind of situationally chicken, what I saw.
I guess that's OK for boys in Orlando, the best of the so great.
You read that article in *Parade* about Cinnabon?
"Yeah,"

Down at the nutritionist's offices, painted all lecithin.
You get hurt, and where are we? In the resort castle complex,
Both of us crying!
This I also later do. And I'm feeling bright brown too,
Too important to acknowledge my own mother's e-delivered
                        storm forecasts, I'll tell you that much.
What she loves she loves because she's dumb,
This'll be the final night of her Indonesian biker gang.

HAIKU

I don't like to be
Seen drinking these intimate,
Brandy concoctions

Alright, so The Devil stars in it as this real terror of a Hollywood musical producer, who goes around, superconducting on each of his pictures, transforming props into weightless slashing glass fragments, pulling baby snake necklaces from jam jars, serving troglodytic coffee – the water in the pot, in actuality, being liquid mercury. Poisonous as hell.

He phones up the employment service and hires himself a new Girl Friday. Not only does he not eat her, they start spending a lot of time together taking care of various errands. She's plucky, thrifty, she's all, "No, don't", and he's all, "You kids can't take this." But as he pays her the dough, she quiets.

In little time, though, through a rich string of events – first of all, the Devil had never once witnessed food being cooked – his employee starts causing all these new insights for him. He'd ascended to Earth with preconceived, even mechanical views! She shows him how lighters work, and they even get through some scenes of *Steamboat Willie* before he melts the projector with his thoughts. Aaaah! He goes.

Still, the Devil begins to take on a bright, new skin. It's forming like Brazilian flora on a Japanese dress. Like its luxury, a "shopper's armor".

Soon after, his assistant takes off on some putrid story arc, she's parachuted into a cool hilly mill-town for a few days, she gets to know some singing ice-delivery guys. Meanwhile, the Devil begins to round up people for auditions, and others to disintegrate! He's a mess. Nobody seems right for the big singing parts in his sombrero epic. He cries distraught in his burning bed, and even the approaching, watchful, servile reptiles cannot placate it.

It's the next morning! Was the Devil dreaming fearfully? He feels fearless now. He resolves to go out and eat an omelet. Sitting alone at the diner counter, his insides are roiling, bad. He gets so sicked, he burns up an entire roadside-attraction community in thoughtless sheets of flaming oil. The characters that were smiling in the big billboard ad beforehand are wheezing and sobbing now!

See? He can't get that shiny kid out of his head. He resolves to immolate the town he sent her to, something to render her home. He's willing up a crazy blast. But not so fast: here they come now, his girl and her suitors!

Their smiles could light up a mine, they rip down the sloped drive through the studio gates on motorbikes with sidecars, their chests heaving with veterans medals. Singing about skiing, about all the blacknesses of heaven.

She's so back! The musical opens in a night! How many guys will hold a rose in their teeth for her? Why is the Devil so angry with Miss Kansas? Why'd he bleed real blood when he nicked himself with the wand towards the end? How could a little kid locked in a black refrigerator make everyone suddenly chuckle?

What were those vampire dogs?!

This is some of the things that happen in *The Devil's Big Bow* (Prod: Wayne Dye, 1938).

CIVIL WAR SIEGE DRESS PATTERNS

About those *Stuperstars*...

What's your plight, tonight's delight?
"How much fuller his box gotta get?"
Wherever the wind smears my snuff.

Civil War is <u>on</u>:
Pleated shores,
But ironic trades,

Ribs of magma, then
Honeyed comas.
Oh I'm not on that thing,

Nobody gonna fist <u>me</u> after we touch land
And I'm <u>not</u> gonna lie in the sandbags again,
Yet it's really touching to hold this other guy!

The supernatural plants around here are all Him...
"I wanna hold your ham."
"Use your zeal to light my cigarettes!"

THY KNIFE

If the girl is
Ardent,

               The bait
               (or *dowry*) is light,
               Says kites to radio,

When those Pansies
Can bomb down on
Our Fraternity, wtf?   105,500,

               This instructor isn't
               Listening at all
               To my pancreas mind.

You're tanked, but
I'm not hating on you
You got a future later

               After you're a
               More consistently
               Online Hip-Hop
               Praducer. I'll see ya!

THE LIGHT CATERER

1.

"I am 'Earn-o'." I,

Uneasy as a lily is, bad at playing
New York sentinel, somehow became a
Major blogger & fan of the City's
Best new ham croissant stores.

This talk about nice places reminds me of Queens,
Where I live, in Central Apartments Point.

If I seem geared up by your courage about moving here,
And am shallow by it for whole days,
Please don't let me be defined
By these trippier moments, mostly
Ash-encased views of an escarpment.

When you come away from the major city
Things always get so muddy-footed.

2.

"Lazy, it's You"

"She'll comp me the two charges"

"But Ah wannabe the asp"

"I might be dying, but I'm not reasonable."
"And this Town Car is dirty."

With our dinosaur artifact flapping
Smoothly out our window, I know
I am worth less than the cavity eaten into it.

3.

Fluttering, like little fish flick it,
With horns coming up on them,
Leviathan carp shades
Hunt the colloid lake.

Even though they've been on
Beer all day, they're jumpy and
Truthfully alive, you can have
Conversation with them for awhile,

Until you are purple to the Limit
(You can't breathe underwater!)

4.

But playing in the Marines orchestra sucks.
You spit once, you hate on John Ritter,
And you're done. 5 of them are
Assigned to ritually beat the
Crap out of you. Then you're made a Reservist,
Dumped down onto a spiked sacrificial floor
1/4 mile under the ground,
After no trial.

HOT FORESTERS

1.

It's what I'll pick up on from
People's totally observable dependings:

Between the peaks of two communicators,
A detailed creek shoots out like the little tongue,

You strive at the interface, having tigerish thoughts,
Broadcast from a ivy hole in your back:

"I love you Sandy!"

2.

It's also the first thing
I ask whenever
I meet a Japanese
Person: "Why Japan?"

3.

Wait, you really want to spend the time
You have left with your mom?

Sorry but you wouldn't put any money up.
Nothing's going to happen. You, dive,

Get back into your pastel Jeep, dick,
You're convicted of pissing on the arts!

4.

C'mon, have it!
Disco of wolfmen,
Burkas of cigars,

Get back,
Get back, Back
Into your pastel Jeep.

5.

Didn't I just say? No.
Miffed lifes are continuously lived,
The team's catcher confirms this –
He's at the perennial back
Of that system's bus,
His ass always hurts, and

You lose yours, but hey you're hardly done,
And nobody else'll find the missing primate now,

Its mouth frozen in agony, distended by a carton
Of Andes Crème de Menthes you got at Costco.

6.

I have to tell you how awed I felt to be standing at the
Undisputed highest point in the Maine State Parks system.

7.

While doing traveling college wildlife shows,
I contracted shoulder cancer.

Judo, you son of a bitch!
And reggae and soccer!

Thankfully, my religion helps me make some noise
                                    about religious issues,
In pleas (structured as moves across airfields)

With Christ descending upon me, his ashes passing
                                    through baker's racks,
Constructed exactly as he had claimed,

From bright birch masts.

SHAKESPEARE

When Romeo made love to Juliet, wouldn't you think his Mom
Got super <u>pissed</u>? Can you just yank a fine young *fromage*
Out of reliable home life that way? Her surrounding
Family seems so adorable, with all their second sight,

I sit on my balcony, nodding about it like everyone else watching.
My hijack open, my mouth shining,
My eyes like adjacent smoke detectors.
Being at those plays really told us the time,

But it was Shakespeare's letters
What convinced me to drive to correspondence school,
Hoping I'd master comedic tap, chase after equipment,
And finish the book about my dad.

No go. Buying my lunch like everybody, trying to fit in, but –
This side of the Food Court? Uh, *I'm all shoot up*.
Poor people look so mean when they're doing laundry.
Two or three kick!

They might even try to operate on Juliet.
Which is like saying, "Choice businesses are stupid." Yeah, I see.
There's 270 million people who voted for Romeo & Juliet
                                        to survive at the end,
Running around after, telling everybody, "Hey, no problem."

I LICK THE WAY

I have now awoken in my crew's house.
It was for real I got cut. No lie yon,
It was my decision from the outset,
As acting 'Master of Dusk'
To those presently here.

You women did me a favor marrying me.
That shit is the onset of itself. They
Made such mountains
Of routines, stuffing me first with tortillas,
Then thoughtfully raised beef,
Pouring over me like cold Sprite.

My own shorts would never come so easily undone,
I wouldn't go for a man's martial hymns, no,
I wouldn't lie down in his persimmon Toyota truck.

DUMPIRE

I felt valuable at that point in the episode, but you have to wonder,
With Rosie and Madam getting it on under the overcoats,
And Raju fully done up – but so wasted, he just drops
Right in the villain's sugar boilers (what dumb traps!)
Would I, the lead, have to fight this alone,
The night glowing bright as beer?

You'd say,
"What should you say when you are introduced to dead strangers?"
"I'll report back to the racists?" No. You'd say, "I'm only baby bait."
Me: "I worked so much tonight, I fainted again."

I'll store your web prints, transfer them to DVD+R, archive it,
Leaving you to focus on village flyovers. This is apparently
Right around when Melinda meets Caleb. He's so brash, so sweet,
He says he grew up watching my TV show at the dump!

PART TWO

I was like,
Sons: How about a prank?

This cat-like dude's family owns a television shop,
He's a father type, a gentleman, but he'll only speak to cats.

You shitty little kids, he goes,
You will have chicken's gills.

I make you rice rolls,
We hurry to vacations,

Tiny lakes area, Koreans videotaping a boat-launch,
Hookers lining the Volcano.

My trick dice demos always start up
Tiresome complaints in the crowd,

Whenever we go to get gas at Chevron,
We're chased away because of The Incident.

I'll never shoplift another ice-mint genital spray
Off those organic juice Indian mofos. It turns out,

Most flowers used in witchcraft don't smell nice,
At all. They manifest their worth with spite,

Forming right up in the
Crotches of God's designs.

Like a typo,
Tough in the trough,

I'm in there by myself, surmounted by Public Art,
And the fakir was toast.

SWAMI

1.

My mommy is a swami,
My uncle is a girl,
The effect drives us off Orchards Road.

Others might think that human-shape carrots
And radishes can also be swamis:
They have got butter in their shit.

Their spy recordings are asinine with fog…totally
Polite, but stressed out with the face veins, like
Physicians sitting before their daily feast of human touches,

All of them swamis!

2.

They're called 'Psionic Mathletes'.
They hear sounds we can't even detect.
Most their habitats got burned by humans.
There's a bunch of them still in a place where
I would definitely need an air-conditioner!

So, what is it about hot Indian girls and young tree-trunks?
"You get one of them up, then you waive the other back down."

3.

It is lightly lit up, compared
To down and over, but there's
Where my girlfriend now lies,
In her dormitory, like a log bench.

Skin tying her guts in, shifting
Water effect moving her bottom out,
And then that top drops down.
Thank you very much, man, I really love her!

4.

Thy lady is cool and glassy as
A primo San Francisco rental unit.
I will have to let her be her,
As she falls out of the back of life.

I can ride most the way up Sansome,
She might as well go work in a mine.
I should trust it and just understand,
Not blot upon her transit,

Laying across her armor of commitments.

POEM

Can I help that I am a woman in my late teens, living right across
from the beer store next one of the main worker entrances at the
mine? And that the only time I can check internet is when I'm
outside on my steps around lunchtime, gettin' naked? And that
I'm also hot deaf and willing and blonde?

WILL WALL

Watery spirit, and a low aerobic
Threshold. Go on add it up.
I don't know, I couldn't deal with my head
Being shaped like the dog god's.
You'd go surfing until lunch, but in a dog costume, and –
They all simply backed into you,
Until you show up on News Five, your
Puppy-boy face superimposed on a map graphic.

Because space is now more like your real life…
You have good Chinese crewmates up there,
But you still yell at them, for clasping their
Hands dangerously behind the back,
Buying up any valuable glazed aluminum dolls,
And methodically going after all our Dad's stuff.

THE HATCH (LOCKUP)

Behind every duck gangster, there's a tightly wrapped
Middle-eastern kid? Maybe ignore that survey.

See: the charred ranch walls prove I was there:
They still smell (warm)

So I got back in my Honda
Instead of going off on her. It didn't all necessarily fly,

I now watch-follow an invisible dog step into a ruined shrine,
Rocking my arms, every day,

Sick of watching the convicts doing intense situps,
I'm gonna shove some runes up that Aryan chick's ass.

GLOW SODA

But I'm from England: there's loads of double-decker
Buses there, filled with <u>punters</u>.
The whole of Britain is just filthy,
A stupa of dying whitened sea-plants.
The English held hands like Roman place-holders,
Their crocodiles became diagonal.
Man I wish I could just coast along,
Crawling out of my problems and
Into a pretty 1940s dress, like they've done at times.

POEM (AFTER SAPPHO)

No tablet, but that in girlfriends,
I always be rooting for them;
My hero chin parts to let in your peerless hair,
Here comes some amazing pussy!

THE POWERFULLY SIMILAR

Glove-like torsos?
I lick the way.

Soul gems and Girl trains,
Black whole, harsh fats,

"She mars all,"
"Legs and feet,"

"Man and Bok Choy."

"As I kiss the Dracula-collared triplets."

THE PART OWNER (PROVINCETOWN)

1.

"You're just a foolish girl character
In milk industry-sponsored playlets
I perform for schools across the Urban Southwest."   "So?"

Frightening variants of turgid nougat,
Yellow, '73, god damn, say
Goodbye to a whole helicopter of bullshit.

I stopped paying my answering service,
I was fuck-startled,
I got newspaper readers into my rentals,

Where when I'd walk in, they'd dive
Under Harry Potter comforters,
Fashioning stacks of muddy 1870s coins in the cunt,

Over unearthly callings, in perfect English
By Patsy, Rosie's (115-year old) bird.
I wouldn't call that renting though.

2.

It's windy, and I'm so caught up in it! I see

White beak boats lie on the lit black water,
Trees sway in muppet costumes, and

Graphite carts of boy witches
Lightly drum on the planks.

Robotic swimmers catch rashes,
Mimic-involving what they endorse-devoured,

Which is totally applicable to the scheme,
And way cooler than touching her books.

3.

Anyway, they'd blow their skyscraper out
By tunneling along its ankles first,

Using the moon's shadow for a bridge,
Which also happens to be the best time for factions.

Track welding, truck-like spitters, the
Beads of soulder on my hardcore memory plunge.

I'm back, and I dig what you did for your planet,
The wind exercising in the hollows of your wet trunks,

I was also asked to co-command as President of Boats,
To sit up in front and to be there with Him,

In that room, with its herm of Eisenhower. It was nice,
The news coming on, everybody soaked.

For walking out on that job because he was so smart,
He was bored by even the most powerful policies,

Thought-transference congresses? To Him,
Those were just old faggots swimming downhill laps.

He'd meet his own friends at Tim's Lamb Pub,
Going, Fuck, what drinks go good with turkey pasta?

By shaking off the animism though, every
Single second of our lives exerted more dynamism,

You could kick anybody you wanted in the hatch.

DICK CARLA ASTRO

1.

Her breasts shot right out her shirt.
I have one of the things instantly

In my jaw. Both her hands drop
Down–

Now she says _Hi_, with
My fingers running up

Over her shoulder like a
Courthouse staircase,

She's a pencil sharpener,
I'm biplanes,

In the fried chicken screening room
Of competitive grabs,

Record-holding, spicy and pacey,
Trenchy.

2. A Warm Night

I later died of big Media, in a castle made of rams,
I went over to L.A., I contracted LAMYDIA.

At competing high-concept kennels,
It rained pawns.

Scan City? Oh, it sure was. And man is it warm there or what?
The downtown is like a heap of steel piñatas,

Erect and sucking their own filth,
I'll tell you that much. I'm usually a

Comanche of hard cotton, but there,
Turning pure blue-raw blanched,

My bosom halved into tiki-torch lit skywalks
Stretched between sustainable residential towers,

An abstract crowd staring at me the second I look up:
I've been talking to a platter of diver scallops this whole time!

3.

Later,
Awed by the influential men,
I put all 13" into the telescope

That chicken I saw that had its limbs and wings
Split out; with garlic and parsley and a char on it.
My god…was it also dead? Oh fuck.

I'll take no further information from your forwarded links.
I guess I expected the representatives of the
15 billion galaxies to sit me down,
One at a time, and just sort of tell me
The unique stories of their whole scene,
Fill me in real quick,
In direct and simple language
Which I could then fashion into professional telecasts.

Wrong: I got idiotic San Diego Chargers facts.
Once those guys' projects go solar, though,
Forget about it, they'll be enthralled by the sun,
Pale and high and mean and low.

Anybody examining the program turns chicken,
All the interesting bits left in the archives get sold,
Your job is fucking de-funct.

But anyways, what, who else did my beach
Culture spaceship drawings piss off?!

4. Celtic Delta

I'm eating the rest of a dead man's frozen carnitas and tacos.
Your thoughts clothe cloudy shadows
in hung long underwear and windy snaps,
Good for you (her).

Poetry's remarkable payouts can enter likably
Through iron nickel slots into my abdomen,
My dome. Economic meaning come to completely help,
As I prepare veggie burgers alongside my associates,

Those are some more guests in the lights of my house.
I been away, see? That's the card, me, still forgetting which
Room of the apartment I'm in, my furnishings morphed
Into gilded sitars that pointlessly face the Nordstrom Outlet,

Which I don't dig, honey! Those grills always go off. Next door,
At the Piano Time, I see this dumb-menacing little kid,
In a brown-white Michael Jackson tribute shirt: where
Michael Jackson was getting eaten by bugs!

THE CRUTCH JOGGER

1.

Half of the up-haul is shiny,
The other half is bug mud.

Lo, it burned through your backpack,

Get some patches made, plot out
Your territories, and start guardin':
Change is a total ho.

2.

Watch out as you ping among the features,
Any of your feelings can get dug up with it,

That job is no park, see
How easy you just say yes?

In the new world, young kids are online gambling,
And ack, they win, by using vitamin go drinks,

That's the thing about leaving your keys behind with toddlers,
While you bike up to the place with the sculptures,

Suddenly you'll have to run off
And go whip your cousin's butt.

I'd rather take a bunch of hits and stare at those kids on the field.
The girls can really block, and man

Are their little – the suits are so dank and stunning.
The moon's hand strike on each grassy strap,

As your poetry goes on military excursions, like a team,
A gigantic penis breaching its ruthless tire.

SPURBANITE.COM

Since 2002,
THE online home for Spurs fanatics from New Braunfels
to Hondo and beyond!

If you're from Comal, Guadalupe or Medina County,
You can WIN great tickets to Spurs home games, or one of SIX
Spinnyhands Full Court Pizza Dinners To-Go! San Antonio ROCKS.

HOLIDAY MEETING MINUTES

– Christmas Elves in the scarlet bunny Spurs mini-dresses
– "Spursosexuals" Should their shirts be ald. in the arena? (Ron)
– Spurbanite: Selling YOUR Service or Product (Spur-oduct!)

Think about THAT, and the REBRAND.

Ron: We now own spurbanite.com, we're up there on the
Alamodome's biggest graphics. But how will we re-ignite our
patented Spurdom with the upcoming fall holiday revenue season?

Jeff: Well Ron, we're gonna do it by dunking the same clear-glass
pumpkinhead ornament Spursketballs we used as the promo in
2005…but now with extensive 3D FX.

Michelle: After these ones get dunked, the cracking Spurs-logo
glass fragments keep breaking down in size, smaller, smaller, until
it resembles fine, cool, blown snow.

Andy: It's a Spurstorm! Tim and Tony feel the cooling effect, and rocket downcourt. Now the snow whirls into an extra ball: and it energizes! They hit simultaneous 3-pointers (double score).

Ron: Big LED's!

Michelle: Everybody's cheering blows the roof off the Alamodome, and Tim and Tony crack up. The spinning laser cowboy boot Spur symbols (CG) fly up in the crowd and explode into powerful horses; these then morph into Holiday deer with Santa hats and our shaking reins animation (CG w/sound)

Jeff: Cut to Lori's video montage of fast, computer-warped legend highlights (6 secs) synced up to the trademark 'explosures' effect (2 secs)

Ron: Friggin' Spurmania personified. This is gonna be a hit spot! Am I right people?!

SPINNYHANDS PIZZA *EL DIABLO* BACKSTORY

Andy: CG opening – pure mozzarella and EL DIABLO® Fire Sauce bubbling in Hell. Echoey voices scream out "The Devil's Pizzaaaaaah!" (flamed graphic)

Dissolve: Satan's in the library at an internet station. Oh no! He got his own online ID, and prints out 35 pages of search results in 9 seconds. Evil pizza research papers fly in the Downtown San Antonio sunset. His recipe info disrupts the whole reference level, backroom shelves quake, then the scaffolding over the new main library building starts to shudder. It goes dark! Basketball courts rip open!

Ron: (CG) Flames like the El Diablo recipe intensity's gonna burn the place down!

CUT to a giant room of prep stations and ovens with little imps working and Devil red pizza paddles dancing around the cooking area. We like Michelle's idea of the "sorcerors apprentice" group broom motion, btw.

Ron: I like that too. Classic.

Suddenly, boom! Blazing kitchen, the oven doors burst open all at once, and there, in gleaming Spurs home whites, Timmy and Tony slip out in a tornado of flames (CG) with lots of glowing, DJ spinning-scratching EL DIABLO PIZZAS!

Andy: Our Cheddar Ranch *ChickInferno* is the best visually, and it's been the best tester too. We put two pages of coupons for it in the Sunday Express News on April 17th, right before the Spurs' second first round home game. We can continue with those on alternate weeks.

Ron: But I wonder, does/can the spot proceed on, to where Timmy and Tony actually do something with these awesome pies? Something sportslike? Let them use the pizzas for shots, which keep traveling down through the air together until they stack up above the rim like a column of Pringles. They drop through the hoop – all three pointers – and maybe the score racking up makes the Jumbotron explode (CG).

Michelle: So now the pizzas are so taste-powerful, they continue on like animated rotating saw-blades, and chase their master the Devil right out of the Alamodome! It turns out "The Devil's Pizzaaaaaah!" was made out of white angels all along! TD and TP make awesome swish gestures: Spurs win! Get ready for summer 'cause it's hot!

Andy: As a finish, the Alamodome flashes with spinning motorcyle-gears, vrooming Spur symbols, subsonic booms, and moans and claps.

CUT to the graphic of North County Spinnyhands locations, as TD and TP and the cute dark-haired kid take little bites out of a flaming slice.

THE GHOULISH WALL DUCKS

Sour salty buttery oily sulfur,
Flamingo with ramen, 2010.

Buildings hooking the perimeter of, this lake
In bakelite circlets

It's about the Mods, and the Deep.

A known baby-girl ghost haunts Jon Acres Pavilion Park,
Its presence often ruins company picnics they hold there,

The crying descending on them like sparklers,
"In hands of smoked turkey"

ARGUING

"There is a light in a pavilion
Over a storied well that will level me up"

"What're you smiling about? You're
Made of rock and your nose got hit off"

"Our room smells like we have
The little electric heater on"

JET BITES

I'm an agent climbing a mountain fortress in a spy book.
I'm a display wall concealing a gang of shootists.
North Korea is firing on my position. I don't plead,

The enticing would tear me outright were it not for my
Neighborhood: every Pole in Hollywood, idly
Radioing his homeboys back at Nestlé Tower
                                        in Tarzana,

Each a clay colossus with a neck of agave. A nemesis.
I'm like, your nemesister. Forget
The dreamy, standoffish reading series
Set in a prominent Syrian eatery,
Run by amazing women who only dig nerve.

Every part of the walk up is a highlight. One
Recites, "I am rice leveling in the sea, kicking wolf ass.
Running off to a pastiche, climber taco place."

BITE JETS

Let me present to you the Parable of the Basketball Batter –

Somehow lured to a mushy barscape,
w/canes pulverizing legs,

Bad in the stance.
Then electrified by a visit to a plain little shop,

Its buttery, transformative chocolate displays,
That seem to keep so well, then suddenly turn specious...

Why give out any effort at all if it(he) could just as easily bail?

SPINNYHANDS
PIZZA TOWN

WORK CRESTS

1.

You out-whimper them for it,
That should overcome their faiths.
Spirit leave me, go to the levee, I go
Leave me, yell at Lee. Lee wants my taco,

Oh his boffo, collapsed molester chest!
I say to my bitch girlfriend
In the Construction Industry.

Good luck then, luck,
Cutting night open into peanuts, she was gone.
Throwing around free condoms from the store,
Eating her chinese Jif!

Is Popeye's Chicken an affordable cure?
I don't yet know.
Matters appear otherwise rabid,

And pregnant, but it wasn't me! I'm a Patholic.
Though, right as I was getting into all
The big free anthologies, my magic arm stopped up,

In our blazing kitchen, done writing,
Dialogue just emanating from my mouth.

2.

"I'll whip my shirt off at a <u>pretty</u> early stage with a girl,
That's how I get with amazing 32-year-old arts programmers.
Instant grand junction,"

"Almost metallic and tall as hell, these girls. I'll tell you though,
Once one comes out from beneath her creator's cowardly overhang,
She's shrieking and jerking back from the shock," I said.

"The flat platinum sun of my <u>talent</u>."

3.

Today's one? She was helpful, sure, but overall, pretty taked.
Some episodes she rallies,
Projects with sense, yeah, and also
Witty, but it dies out, I'm just, sorry,
She seems way more watched than used.

Behind the tears, we're more good. You agree!
It's a sweet pie we've filled w/tart insiders' perspective.
You'd rather put on cleats and I would too,
So me and you can get up on the dome. Hey, I'm afraid,

Couldn't you just as easily help me kick in panels
For an amazing sauna we'd plan and build together?
Only to turn abruptly around, totally crying again.

OLD MILWAUKEE

You kids need to quit being so meek about your resp. upsides,
Walk away from the bowling alley & start writing up those
                                    extraordinary claims.

It was some decent, fair times for the most part I had.
Your room decorations though?
I bet pretty High German. God-y.

Were they always? You know,

I met with one once, "in a beer volcano."
"A Miracula." "An enthrall-cano."

I am. I am. Go,

"Wait, is Ganesh the one that loves getting drunk?"
"No, but that's a god I like a lot though!" "Oh!"

VISTA

Oily seas and D-battery reefs, basic Kabul.
Mudslide bushes, bricks of butter, slabs of idea:

The rib eye. Overthought chai-sandwich places,
Dale killed off, Gonzo posed.

"Tropism?"
Advice scurries back from debit,

Ottoman arcs
Rotating to the forces,

I'm still keeping my Prada stuff,
Even after it got melted.

Like jet pistols secreted inside
World-famous performance harps,

I faked all that other imagery, but (I
Think) I fabricated it fairly,

Epistolary and scary, go
Take me to the Taco Bear.

Using my arms to fly to farms, where
The flowers cling bizarrely to their beds,

Petals opening up into detailed camouflaged guys:
You brainiacs'll have to live with that instead.

CHANG AND ENGLISH

Shame the dog had to leave, let alone
Its classic friend. Not two seconds of ceremony
And the thing's over on its back,

A mid-20th century pictorialist church
Drenched in cheesy posters about AIDS.
Photoreal homes, stuffed with iron bling,

With no dirt doorway to stand behind, I'm
Shucking a box of corn and staring at
The yellow eyes I reveal!

Bermed octagons up-respond in white glow,
Sheer sedans of notes, their status oscillated,
Simon haunting Simon.

CHERIMOYA

The Presidio clue.
Giant seeded marrow quads, party walls
Streaked by saturated aquatic green colors,
Steps of bronze, and you.

Eyeing the bye, shaky in gowns,
The will divides shipping into lanes,
Steel-hulled boats, they go straight down,
And our Lad towers in the veins.

His dancing won't be ageless,
In weather of furious issues,
The night my husband gets clipped.
"I didn't like those triangles on their gauges,"

So I say, What's up with leather?
Rain makes the outside so warped and tender
And thin, like penis skin. After,
All you can do is stand around during the song.

IKE KELLY

OK, I'll be calm. Even though
I'm a hostage in a helicopter,
<u>Again</u>.

Go ahead, captors, call me "whale": not funny!
Most whales are at least <u>really active</u>,
If not <u>completely majestic</u> and <u>inspirational</u>.

Your mother and your
Aunt have paid $55-$90 multiple
Times to take a ferry out into

Freezing, shit conditions to <u>maybe</u> see
Whales
Whales

Whales.
You know it!
You fuckin' suck 4 evah!

MELLOW ACTIONS

1.

Here comes your son, with a white scarf tied nicely around his face.

2.

The powerful family story becomes a shitty ride.

3.

Silly Robots: Real Moms.

4.

To those DC-area kidney donors on strike: break it off!

5.

When the Mongols are disappointed, they usually
Won't tell you what you did and didn't do right.

6.

Try and be the larger parent in their drawings.

7.

You did every bad thing that David Bowie did.
But have you had any positive
Contributions at David Bowie's level?
You haven't, Skip.
Now shut up about your David Bowie!

8.

Anybody recall some song about a good general contractor?

9.

Nobody asks the photographer about her paintings.

10.

Funny Pampers   Pizza Quiet.

11.

The sweetest-faced kid ever approached me, whispering,
'Let me tell you about how awful it is to do robberies.'

12.

You scored,
Now come off that goddamn field.

13.

Should you be patient with doctor?

14.

Do you necessarily always have to do what you heard?!

15.

Enroll in a communist high school, then watch yourself really
Phase out. Those textbooks are just forested in what-ifs.

16.

And dynamic language: quit aiming it.

17.

Move him with pitches so he'll have to keep
His little body entirely away. Too abrupt,
No chance. I'd call low. Like you'd go!

18.

Don't be suddenly hesitant now,
March up there like a hero in your bat-black gunner armor,
Kick up them lightning-enhanced dragon pumps.

19.

Better comic actors will work more orange into their hair.
I just want to forewarn you.

20.

An Italian stop-motion animated duck smoking narrow,
'Capri' cigarettes.

21.

Just go for a jog and wait for the bull crap to pan out.

22.

What do old people like?
Silent movies, three per worn-out videocassette,
About frightened poor persons.

23.

Floral and choral on
The flower and choir.

24.

I am stayed pure.

25.

Pour gravel on a poet's grave
When you find a poet's grave,
Then go to the bathroom on the gravel.
Poets are dipshits!

DWELL–E

1.

Our Discovery Store Annex is a tiny little place,
Fitted out with thorny wigwams and aluminum beams,
Kind of stained, basic for the Plaza,
With shirts for explorers, and thermoses. But
There's a sensational digital hammock on display,

Suspended from galvanized,
Weaved cables, it rocks like a porch swingset,
Along exquisite, charged tracks,
Holistically reacting to all kinds of stimuli,
Due to its latticed solar design.

2.

I gazed upon the buildings of Doom IV…
And the corners of my eyes stung…I was for the thing.

One guard gave me two incredible earrings,
Like a kind of good-bye gratuity. I carried
Them with me for months, all across the
U.S.S.S.S.S.S.S.S.

Past multiple checkpoints,
Up in my doo.

"Tears for Ears," for
Fruits of the ocean given unsurpassed leeway,

Red spilled out on white shoulders,
The caca arriving in the courtroom.

3.

Now ashy-face synthetic dudes,
"Hold Nike cameras in their butt."

"I know,"
Wandering the corridors like Harrier Jump-Jets,

Rolling in the aether with Tom Snyder,
While Queen Latifah bartends for the Country Bears.

4.

Reap. Eat.
My night is yuck –

The fever for noodles
Finally hit a pond (clawed)

Your heart and lips in a trope fugue,
Seeing Zorro's head twisting funny around the neck.

His flange lands on the deck and compresses,
The nightscape living and also dead,

But, while the same-sex thing
Is initially a heap of fluttering,

Followed by a general hunkering down,
They can later get taciturn as time.

Reserving velvety night inns online, but so conservative
At the bash itself, as though there was no us in the USA.

POEM

"Hey, whatever happened to Roy Clark?"

He had the ability to float through the sky.
I recently learned he drowned in a 8" deep creek.

So much for that guy's wishes

For those dykes,
They went up and died down.

"They wash their sweaters so much,"

Says an insensitive world
Breaching over the ants,

Pissed off at him,

Begging to be punched.
Like a virgin.

SALT JOG (NY)

My Dad puts on his russet tracksuit and takes off.
Bugs in trees, come out! He says, not waiting,
Right away he pauses,
In conscientious charge.
Standing in a wheatfield sporting cherry-pattern shorts,
Before a fussy, ill-will energy plant,
Protesting the canon.

It's the core of the back-pain of our startup,
Creepy partitions shaped by an
Insurmountably tense, insectoid drive,
Heroic ministries caught behind the deer fence.
Do I wonder if I'm one? It depends. I'm not waiting,
Nutritious sprays make a deadly dusk, so we just run.
I think my Dad's a hawk foam gun.

SOMETIMES, ON MY SHOULDERS, ARE HER PANTIES

1.

Together since they were temple kids,
Nude and obsessed with country music,

Having a great day out at Wheat Ridge,
Too bad I couldn't escape from the well by force.

The ex-Little Rascal had an amazing rack,
And was disarmingly sociable,

She kissed me all over my ears, even though they
Both looked like sombreros made from old pie crust.

2.

Once the blood is draining out the head,
Is survival really that freq? It's gonna
Be over pretty much, there's
All kinds of things you coulda done to yourself.
1–2–3–5, dead, your eyes fixated
On her Red Rancho t-shirt.

3.

The favor that I'm asking of you now

Is a collage of previous favors
I've been previously granted by (*insert .xl file*)

Easy, normal ones.
Get over your cat's death!

Stop claiming to be "altered" now, to being
500 guns wired to a fuse array,

In the hay loft, hidden by protruding bright
Iron racks, hoping nobody up there is a Kraut.

Emptily cannoning into junkie teen torsos,
Is there a better onramp toward the self?

It is what wood looks like when it dies,
Like a spitfire college with soul-sucking brown windows!

BAKERY IN A RIVER

Luau vats…softcore tree scene.
A furious American beer

For an All-American bear,
The darts pumping into Kermit.

A better editor
Could empty out my project's entire sepsis

Mine flies when he could walk,
Skillfully popping up locked in place, soon to gone.

We really hope he gets back working at Stardump,
After being so miserable on Pong Mtn.

TOMÁSZ HÖRTL

I want your little dog to quit scratching up my fruit trees,
But no, wait, I guess you're probably busy banging your
New clinician boyfriend right about now.
I hope you boys jump in each other's bagels,
And inscribe 'all I want' on the hollow
Insides of your little penises. I'm telling everybody,

But whatever I say about Teddy's wife, who has a dick too,
My own wife is still just a 4' 4" dwarf thug,
All tatted up and down her cane arm. What panegyric?!
She's probably shoplifting right now at the Safeway,
Stowing tri-tip under her mealy hoodie. But get off it,
My angel still has her dreams going strong,
These constantly moving hills she depicts with paints,
200-300 people partying up on Glacier Exit Road.

NIL FACE

Magic makes for noiseless graves,
And oily demoiselles.

At the lab promos they rave,
Sit there and perm-harden like elms.

Was there a chance
They'd glance

Down the slope
Toward the tower of teeth?

Shouts in
Chalky diaper hells.

SHYAWN

You know, I believe I've banged a girl from every country
Represented by the flags on our young child's kite.
Planets are sex planets in Zodiac roles.

Saturnus does <u>what</u>? Sponsors <u>what</u>?
Human life was cleaved off the carjacker molecule,
What a tight main ingredient to derive from,
Intensive summer interactions,
But so much snowing in the videogames!
The liar starts to automatically lean back,
Bulky, pointy, pretending to enjoy a personal letter
In his own language <u>that he can't even read</u>.

I'd rather be kicking new ideas around with my partner,
Just me and Shawn and our Camcorder.
The hairy legs scoot across the Lab.

POEM

I made good on a big art-school vow,
In 1995. That April,
We chained up all these old
Teachers and starved them.
Later on, the teachers were set
Loose on some weak-willed,
Overweight third-grade kids.
They outwitted the kids pretty
Quickly, drove them into corrals,
And cooked and devoured them.
The following morning,
They finished the cold remains.

Then they carefully strung the victims' bones together
Weaved with intestinal viscera, and bush branches.
This grisly construct would serve as a
Bridge across the silver waterfall and
Rush, granting the filthy instructors passage
Into the lands of the Priesten-Karl.

POEM

1.

Like showgirls sinking into the sea,
Those dogs shit on me, and owned me!

After I came to, I got the 'Nepali Handshake.'
It took how many hours getting the butter off my shirt?!

I've really hurt my own chances to stay with
The stars and burn with the rivers,
Which is why nobody reads my tangential
Hysterical etc. (!)

2.

Moving quickly up the body,
As our lips shriek, "shark!"

But then the shark goes, "Fellas!"

SEA-BEAR

1.

Artistic locked-ness!
Pouty European school viruses
Coming onto our ruby emerald Christmas,
Boldly laying their cars down before your Dad.

He thinks, Shit! Help, whatever, polio. End-times.
FACE YOUR CHASER, I would've proudly said,
Icily grown, doin' roofing up in the Cascades, vitriolic;
Seeing pearled, jewelly, holed-by-bullets light sources,

Then reaching down for my buddy, thinking,
"There goes everything that got me sad."

2.

If I fail to avenge his death of you
Two guys, throw bricks at my head!

I am the one that created the
Ice-Dancing Sasquatch Footage. I originated it,

With serene dispatches to heavenly space, by digital wagon,
Watching all those young girls go so far at the Olympics.

3.

Like a laser pointer, over the gray sea,
I put my helicopter down in your library courtyard.
How hot am I? Well, I only pretend to love
                         these really rich dudes,
Though that for some reason is polarizing.
Don't hate me because I'm delicious.

Few attentions in the state park are more cherished.
I've had big programs in more than 150 stores,
Now I feel the sections.

4.

The Etchings?

Renaissance portraits
Of standing house-cats in
Bright Tuscan mercenary armor, or less

Popular paintings of warheads, vividly scratched
Onto apes. Buckets of blown glass. What?

5.

Which way could I get repetitive sets of
Four of my arm and wing feathers
To, on their own, tighten and form into
Stretched arcs, launching from my
Locked back, evenly spaced, towards a
Progressive storm.
That shit was digital.

If you hadn'tve lashed out at me,
I would of become…
What did you just say? An alligator stripper?
Omar? You really need to stop
Working the kind of jobs they had in 1960!

LOVE SONGS FOR DRIED STACKED TREE-TRUNKS

I'll now close this (my) book and get out of here.
While decent seen from a distance,
You humans are still scum

If you don't like it, that fact, take your
Fucking money back and try swimming
Out of this submarine

So you spent about thirty bucks on brunch.
I don't care about Brooklyn: I unhear its reader votes.
Brooklynites are like trendy urban Swedes circa 1984-1985

"But don't knock its Elsinore acoustics."
"And many of their concepts are still on the see-saw, yo."
 Put it in my blini…you Brooklyn bitches.

POEM

Mom and little kid shut down her iMac.
Thank god the dumb people in her book have died!

GEL BED

Wishing you wore a magical collar too.

Sort-of touch my forearm while I look at your titties.

I dunno, I guess this girl sounds alright.
But the messagery in her work makes me rolf,
She can't set nothing to normal speech speed.

Frequently ugly spasms, but also some honest zaps.
4.1 Stars out of 5 Stars

WORM

I can't even mumble, so I kick my
'Legs' back behind me,
Pumping, right-left, pulling
Gathering grabs and bites
Of all the wet dense
Soil I can take that
I spit aspects right back out
Roiling the underground
At the high end of my repeats,
Parading, paving, pushing,
Self sent back through unhealing space, through
Worm holes, making hysterical purpose.

THE ITALIANS

Don't make me eat no little $31 pizza that tastes burnt

Some meal that lived in the dick of Frank Sinatra's cunt.

 has a mission to redefine the terms of accessibility by publishing challenging writing distinguished by idiosyncrasy and intelligence rather than by allegiance with camps, schools, or cliques. It is part of our press's mission to support writers who might otherwise have difficulty being recognized because their work doesn't answer to either the mainstream or to recognizable modes of experimentation.

The Motherwell Prize is an annual series that offers publication of a first or second book of poems by a woman, as well as a one thousand dollar cash prize.

The Fence Modern Poets Series is open to poets of any gender and at any stage of career, and offers a one thousand dollar cash prize in addition to book publication.

For more information about either prize, or more informatin about Fence, visit www.fenceportal.org.

The Motherwell Prize

Negro League Baseball	Harmony Holiday
living must bury	Josie Sigler
Aim Straight at the Fountain and Press Vaporize	Elizabeth Marie Young
Unspoiled Air	Kaisa Ullsvik Miller

The Alberta Prize

The Cow	Ariana Reines
Practice, Restraint	Laura Sims
A Magic Book	Sasha Steensen
Sky Girl	Rosemary Griggs
The Real Moon of Poetry and Other Poems	Tina Brown Celona
Zirconia	Chelsey Minnis

Fence Modern Poets Series

The Other Poems	Paul Legault
Nick Demske	Nick Demske
Duties of an English Foreign Secretary	Macgregor Card
Star in the Eye	James Shea
Structure of the Embryonic Rat Brain	Christopher Janke
The Stupefying Flashbulbs	Daniel Brenner
Povel	Geraldine Kim
The Opening Question	Prageeta Sharma
Apprehend	Elizabeth Robinson
The Red Bird	Joyelle McSweeney

National Poetry Series

A Map Predetermined and Chance	Laura Wetherington
The Network	Jena Osman
The Black Automaton	Douglas Kearney
Collapsible Poetics Theater	Rodrigo Toscano

Anthologies & Critical Works

Not for Mothers Only: Contemporary Poets on Child-Getting & Child-Rearing
Catherine Wagner & Rebecca Wolff, editors

A Best of Fence: The First Nine Years, Volumes 1 & 2
Rebecca Wolff and Fence Editors, editors

Poetry

88 Sonnets	Clark Coolidge
A Book Beginning What and Ending Away	Clark Coolidge
Mercury	Ariana Reines
Cœur de Lion	Ariana Reines
June	Daniel Brenner
English Fragments / A Brief History of the Soul	Martin Corless-Smith
The Sore Throat & Other Poems	Aaron Kunin
Dead Ahead	Ben Doller
Lake Antiquity	Brandon Downing
My New Job	Catherine Wagner
Stranger	Laura Sims
The Method	Sasha Steensen
The Orphan & Its Relations	Elizabeth Robinson
Site Acquisition	Brian Young
Rogue Hemlocks	Carl Martin
19 Names for Our Band	Jibade-Khalil Huffman
Infamous Landscapes	Prageeta Sharma
Bad Bad	Chelsey Minnis
Snip Snip!	Tina Brown Celona
Yes, Master	Michael Earl Craig
Swallows	Martin Corless-Smith
Folding Ruler Star	Aaron Kunin
The Commandrine & Other Poems	Joyelle McSweeney
Macular Hole	Catherine Wagner
Nota	Martin Corless-Smith
Father of Noise	Anthony McCann
Can You Relax in My House	Michael Earl Craig
Miss America	Catherine Wagner

Fiction

Prayer and Parable: Stories	Paul Maliszewski
Flet: A Novel	Joyelle McSweeney
The Mandarin	Aaron Kunin